the everyman series

being God's man...
by standing firm under pressure

Stephen Arterburn

Kenny Luck & Todd Wendorff

WATERBROOK
PRESS

BEING GOD'S MAN...BY STANDING FIRM UNDER PRESSURE

All Scripture quotations, unless otherwise indicated, are taken from the *Holy Bible, New International Version*®. NIV®. Copyright © 1973, 1978, 1984 by International Bible Society. Used by permission of Zondervan Publishing House. All rights reserved.

Trade Paperback ISBN 978-1-57856-918-2
eBook ISBN 978-0-307-55175-7

Published in association with the literary agency of Alive Communications, Inc., 7680 Goddard Street, Suite 200, Colorado Springs, CO 80920.

Published in the United States by WaterBrook, an imprint of the Crown Publishing Group, a division of Penguin Random House LLC, New York.

WATERBROOK® and its deer colophon are registered trademarks of Penguin Random House LLC.

147268265

contents

SMALL-GROUP RESOURCES

welcome to the every man Bible study series

As Christian men, we crave true-to-life, honest, and revealing Bible study curricula that will equip us for the battles that rage in our lives. We are looking for resources that will get us into our Bibles in the context of mutually accountable relationships with other men. But like superheroes who wear masks and work hard to conceal their true identities, most of us find ourselves isolated and working alone on the major issues we face. Many of us present a carefully designed public self while hiding our private self from view. This is not God's plan for us.

Let's face it. We all have trouble being honest with ourselves, particularly in front of other men.

As developers of a men's ministry, we believe that many of the problems among Christian men today are direct consequences of an inability to practice biblical openness—being honest about our struggles, questions, and temptations—and to connect with one another. Our external lives may be in order, but storms of unprocessed conflict, loss, and fear are eroding our resolve to maintain integrity. Sadly, hurting Christian men are flocking to unhealthy avenues of relief instead of turning to God's Word and to one another.

We believe the solution to this problem lies in creating opportunities for meaningful relationships among men. That's why we designed this Bible study series to be thoroughly interactive. When a man practices biblical openness with other men, he moves from secrecy to candor, from isolation to connection, and from pretense to authenticity.

Kenny and Todd developed the study sessions at Saddleback Church in Lake Forest, California, and at King's Harbor Church in Redondo Beach, California, where they teach men's Bible studies. At these studies, men hear an outline of the Bible passage, read the verses together, and then answer a group discussion question at their small-group tables. The teaching pastor then facilitates further discussion within the larger group.

This approach is a huge success for many reasons, but the key is that, deep down, men really do want close friendships with other guys. We don't enjoy living on the barren islands of our own secret struggles. However, many men choose to process life, relationships, and pressures individually because they fear the vulnerability required in small-group gatherings. *Suppose someone sees behind my carefully constructed image? Suppose I encounter rejection after revealing one of my worst sins?* Men willingly take risks in business and the stock market, sports and recreation, but we do not easily risk our inner lives.

Many church ministries are now helping men win this battle, providing them with opportunities to experience Christian male companionship centered in God's Word. This study series aims to supplement and expand that good work around the country. If these lessons successfully reach you, then they will also reach every relationship and domain that you influence. That is our heartfelt prayer for every man in your group.

how to use this study guide

As you prepare for each session, first review the **Key Verse** and **Goals for Growth,** which reveal the focus of the study at hand. Discuss as a group whether or not you will commit to memorizing the Key Verse for each session. The **Head Start** section then explains why these goals are necessary and worthwhile. Each member of your small group should complete the **Connect with the Word** section *before* the small-group sessions. Consider this section to be your personal Bible study for the week. This will ensure that everyone has spent some time interacting with the biblical texts for that session and is prepared to share responses and personal applications. (You may want to mark or highlight any questions that were difficult or particularly meaningful so you can focus on those during the group discussion.)

When you gather in your small group, you'll begin by reading aloud the **Head Start** section to remind everyone of the focus for the current session. The leader will then invite the group to share any questions, concerns, insights, or comments arising from their personal Bible study during the past week. If your group is large, consider breaking into subgroups of three or four people (no more than six) at this time.

Next, get into **Connect with the Group,** starting with the **Group Opener**. These openers are designed to get at the heart of each week's lesson. They focus on how the men in your group relate to the passage and topic you are about to discuss. The group leader will read aloud the opener for that week's session and then facilitate interaction on the **Discussion Questions** that follow. (Remember: Not everyone has to offer an answer for every question.)

Leave time after your discussion to complete the **Standing Strong** exercises, which challenge each man to consider, *What's my next move?* As you openly express your thoughts to the group, you'll be able to hold one another accountable to reach for your goals.

Finally, close in **prayer,** either in your subgroups or in the larger group. You may want to use this time to reflect on and respond to what God has done in your group during the session. Also invite group members to share their personal joys and concerns, and use this as "grist" for your prayer time together.

By way of review, each lesson is divided into the following sections:

To be read or completed *before* the small-group session:
- **Key Verse**
- **Goals for Growth**
- **Head Start**
- **Connect with the Word** (home Bible study: 30-40 minutes)

To be completed *during* the small-group session:
- Read aloud the **Head Start** section (5 minutes)
- Discuss personal reaction to **Connect with the Word** (10 minutes)
- **Connect with the Group** (includes the **Group Opener** and discussion of the heart of the lesson: 30-40 minutes)
- **Standing Strong** (includes having one person pray for the group; challenges each man to take action: 20 minutes)

in search of a spine

She's cute. Really cute. You had no business returning her eye flutters with a smile, but you did. *What in the world are you doing?* asks the voice inside. Images of your wedding, your wife, and your kids flash across your brain. *You're on a business trip— alone,* says the dark side. Fight or flight?

The conversation turns volcanic on the basketball court, and you let this big hulk know, in very colorful language, just how you feel. He's dropping the ball and walking straight toward you with fiery eyes. Fight or flight?

You just aren't getting through to her. She's dug in. You're dug in. You've both made the usual "you always" accusations and "if only you would just" statements. But now you are way beyond taking jabs at each other. Low blows are being thrown. Fight or flight?

Fight or flight? When you're faced with an imminent threat, your body releases adrenaline, your heart beats faster, your brain activity skyrockets, your muscles tense, and all your senses switch to "Go." When does this usually happen to you?

No doubt you could add a half-dozen of your own tense scenarios to the descriptions above. At times like these you know you'll have to make a decision that's crucial to your spiritual health: Will I stand strong in my desire to do God's will or will I run for the hills?

Sometimes the situation is a matter of life or death. Like the guy in the oncologist's office who watches as the doctor lowers his glasses, closes the medical chart, and says, "Your wife's biopsy came back, and I'm afraid you're both in for a long, difficult journey." But will you really be there with your wife every step of the way?

So many tests of our faith! Trials have a way of inspecting our hearts and exposing what's really there. They can either perfect our faith or produce sin. It all depends on how we choose to respond to them.

Let's be honest. The faith path is tough traveling. Fighting to hold on to God's purposes under adverse conditions can feel inconvenient and counterintuitive. But pressure reveals our true convictions about God, about everything in life. Heat reveals the substance of a man. When we stand firm under pressure, we show that we really believe what we say we believe.

In this study we're going to look at four men who show us how we can stand our ground under pressure and not compromise our beliefs.

Daniel and his friends Shadrach, Meshach, and Abednego were innocent bystanders caught up in circumstances beyond their control—a lifelong captivity in a foreign land. But they didn't let misfortune, temptation, manipulation, intimidation, or even death shake their faith. Instead of compromising, they faced each new challenge with courage and trust in God. They didn't use circumstances or the sins of others as excuses for failure. Rather, they kept making choices consistent with their faith, trusting that God would take each situation and use it for His purposes. Their fierce loyalty to God in a pagan culture is what we admire most about them.

As we study Daniel's life, we'll see that obeying God, refusing to compromise, and maintaining our boundaries under pressure is the way to bring Him glory—and will even preserve our own souls. But walking this path is not easy. In today's culture, fleeing when the pressure is on is an art form for most Christian men. Their fight is gone. Comfort trumps godly conviction and loyalty.

Our goal in this study is to stimulate personal reflection and honest dialogue with God and with other men about these issues. As you work through each session, look in the mirror at your own life and ask yourself some hard questions. Whether you are doing this study individually or in a group, realize that being completely honest with yourself, with God, and with others will produce the greatest growth.

Our prayer is that you will become a man of God like Daniel, who was loyal and didn't compromise his faith under pressure. May you increasingly choose to live a life of radical obedience to God and His will. As you do, you'll see that mighty miracles are still available to those who dare to trust Him.

not budging

Staying Loyal to God by Setting and Maintaining Boundaries

Key Verse

Daniel resolved not to defile himself with the royal food and wine, and he asked the chief official for permission not to defile himself this way. (Daniel 1:8)

Goals for Growth

- Set boundaries ahead of time to protect my faith.
- Take proactive steps with people to maintain these boundaries.
- Trust that God will honor my commitment.

Head Start

Nowhere in men's lives are boundaries more needed than in the area of sex. Just think of the disasters that could have been avoided if a few simple rules had been scrawled in fluorescent ink across the canvas of men's minds. We all need to adopt a "Caution: Flammable!" attitude toward sex by establishing healthy sexual boundaries. This is the only way we can keep our commitments to God and to the women to whom we've promised our exclusive loyalty.

But what happens when we fail to decide ahead of time where we will and will not go, what we will and will not do, what we will and will not put before our eyes? We end up killing our integrity and damaging our walk with Christ.

The fact is, we often don't count the cost of spiritual success the way we so naturally do in other endeavors. Players on Wall Street know that if they cross predetermined securities laws and ethical boundaries, they'll be prosecuted (ask Martha Stewart). In sports, everyone recognizes that unless they play by the rules, they will be disqualified. Olympic swimmers know they can't compete unless they swim within their lanes. Tour de France bikers recognize they'll never get a chance to wear the yellow jersey if they take short cuts—or use drugs. And boxers understand that if they punch below the belt, they'll receive penalty deductions.

Here's the deal: God has set predetermined boundaries for men. We not only need to acknowledge the rules and boundaries He's set, but we need to integrate them into our lives.

Daniel understood that he had to set some boundaries in order to remain faithful to God. He knew what the culture was going to throw at him and prepared himself in advance. He knew that for his faith to survive and thrive in captivity, he had to do two things. First, he had to be the best at whatever he did. He had to exceed the expectations of a narcissistic king and earn his respect. Second, he needed to anticipate the cultural practices that would threaten His faith in God so that he could set boundaries without jeopardizing his life. A tall order? Absolutely. But Daniel didn't budge or bend. Instead, he set creative boundaries and trusted God to take care of the rest. And as we'll see, God honored Daniel's strong convictions.

Connect with the Word

Read Daniel 1.

1. Be Daniel for a moment. Why do you feel compelled to set a boundary with the food you're offered (verse 8)? How would eating the king's food compromise your faith?

2. If Daniel had wanted to indulge himself, what excuse or rationalization could he have used?

3. After Daniel presented his request to the king's official, how did God show him that He was at work in the situation (verse 9)?

4. How did Daniel respond when his request came under fire?

5. What does Daniel's response to the official tell us about Daniel, his faith, and his confidence in God?

6. At the end of the ten-day trial period, how did God show His favor toward Daniel for taking this radical step of faith (verse 15)?

7. What do you think God thought of Daniel's initiative in this situation?

8. What impact do you think Daniel's boldness had on the official in charge of Daniel and his friends?

9. Based on verses 18-20, what did Daniel learn from this experience about setting solid, godly boundaries in a hostile environment?

10. What do you learn from Daniel's example in this passage about not compromising under pressure?

Connect with the Group

Group Opener

Read the group opener aloud and discuss the questions that follow.

(Suggestion: As you begin your group discussion time in each of the following sessions, consider forming smaller groups of three to six men. This will allow more time for discussion and give everyone an opportunity to share their thoughts and struggles.)

My (Kenny's) friend (and former UCLA Bruin) Brian Goodell is a swimming icon in my hometown of Orange County, a hotbed for the sport. Brian is frequently asked to speak to audiences about how he won the gold medal at the 1972 and 1976 Olympic Summer Games in the 1,500-meter and 400-meter freestyle events. His performance in Munich and Montreal, he says, reflected years of preparation, thousands of hours in the pool, and a commitment to be the best.

But what if, as Brian crouched at the starting blocks of those events, the black lines and rope lanes were missing as the gun sounded? Splashing, bumping, confusion, and chaos would reign as a half-dozen elite swimmers churned up the water. We all know that an open pool wouldn't work in a race for the gold medal. Individual success requires roped-off lanes. The strength, the heart, the training, the motivation, and the will to succeed *still require boundaries* if they are to produce an Olympic medal.

Many men I know swim and paddle through life without lanes. They may have the desire. They may be well-trained in spiritual disciplines. They may have been studying God's Word and building spiritual muscle by connecting with other men in the church. But when it comes down to putting all this dedication, training, and activity together to win their spiritual races, they pull up short of the finish line.

What keeps many men dog-paddling is their inability to establish the necessary boundaries that take advantage of their training. Just as my friend Brian could not have won his gold medals without lanes, God's man cannot win his battles without boundaries. Flailing away in the water will never be enough; a specific plan needs to be drawn up and pursued. This means laying out, *in advance,* those actions that will preserve your commitment, help you practice your faith, and allow you to produce the desired results you are seeking as God's man.

What could some of those boundaries be? Consider:

- places you will or will not go
- things you will or will not place before your eyes
- friendships you will or will not keep

- situations you will embrace or avoid
- disciplines you will or will not pursue
- words you will or will not use
- conversations you will or will not participate in
- relationships you will or will not pursue
- thoughts you will or will not allow yourself to feed upon
- values you will or will not teach to your kids

In a more specific sense, predetermined boundaries may include deciding to take actions such as these:

- blocking the pay-per-view option at the hotel front desk
- refusing to make low-blow putdowns during marital disagreements
- saying no when asked to do things on weekends that don't involve the whole family
- never being alone with a woman who is not your wife
- turning the channel when there's gratuitous skin on the tube
- deciding that bars will not be your place for meeting women
- refusing to keep self-destructive secrets from your wife
- never making a significant financial or family decision without first consulting your wife

When we deal with these issues ahead of time, we create the lanes in which we can freely allow our spiritual energies to work. We are counting the cost of what it will take to build a solid spiritual life; we are adjusting our expectations to match the reality of being God's man.[1]

---

1. Stephen Arterburn and Kenny Luck, *Every Man, God's Man* (Colorado Springs: WaterBrook, 2003), 197-98.

Discussion Questions

a. The quotation above speaks of men who paddle through life without clearly defined lanes. In what ways are you that kind of man? In what ways are you not that kind of man?

b. Review the bulleted lists in the Group Opener that identify the boundaries men can set in their lives. Which boundaries are most appealing to you? Why?

c. In what specific area(s) of your life are you most tempted to forgo preset boundaries? Why do you think you are most vulnerable in these areas?

d. How could your men's group help you with setting boundaries in these area(s)?

e. What would not budging in these areas look like for you in everyday, practical terms?

f. What gives us the motivation to accept the limits our faith places on us?

g. What is the connection between trusting God and setting boundaries?

Standing Strong

In what primary area of your life are you tempted to compromise?

What boundaries do you need to set for yourself in that area as soon as possible? To whom will you give permission to ask you how you're doing in this area on an ongoing basis?

not panicking

*Maintaining Strong Convictions
and Confidence in Times of Chaos*

Key Verse

Then Daniel went to Arioch, whom the king had appointed to execute the wise men of Babylon, and said to him, "Do not execute the wise men of Babylon. Take me to the king, and I will interpret his dream for him." (Daniel 2:24)

Goals for Growth

- Remember that God is in control of seemingly out-of-control situations.
- Strengthen my faith in God's ability to work in the situation.
- Be willing to be used by God as a central part of His solution to the problem.

Head Start

Most of us men don't do unplanned circumstances very well. We prefer the predictable and the routine. We like to count on maple bars from the donut-shop guy every morning, the kids' soccer practice at 4:00 p.m. twice a week, church every Sunday, work from nine to five on weekdays, and TV shows on the same day at the same time every week. We pray for the sun to rise and shine on our routines, every day, without fail.

What we tend to forget is that earth can be a very unpredictable environment. Your wife's x-ray might reveal a mass in her breast. Your company can tank without notifying you. You can get rear-ended or carjacked at a stoplight. Your identity can be stolen. You can even be taken prisoner to a foreign country and forced into service in the palace of a crazy king!

Okay, that last scenario probably won't happen in your lifetime, but it wasn't uncommon in Daniel's day for conquered peoples to be indentured by their captors. I'm sure that when Daniel was a little boy, he never dreamed of seeing his country destroyed or being thrown into a boot camp for teenagers.

No. It's more likely that Daniel was training to be a leader in Israel. He was well schooled and came from nobility. So imagine what was going through his mind on the death walk from Jerusalem to Babylon after his home had been pillaged. Having survived this first test of his faith, he must have felt as comfortable as anyone could feel being a hostage in a foreign land. He was gainfully employed in a palace, after all. And his crazy boss at least appreciated him.

Then out of nowhere came a news flash: "King's Dream Uninterpretable. Furious King Issues Decree: All Wise Men to Be Executed!"

Hmm. Didn't see that one coming!

Pretend you're Daniel for a moment. What are your options in this situation? Fight? That would be futile. Flight? Gonna need a chariot. Or go to the king, buy some time, promise to interpret the dream, and get your men's group to pray like mad for you?

Connect with the Word

Read Daniel 2.

1. What was Daniel's initial reaction to the king's decree (verses 14-15)?

2. What does Daniel model for us in his initial response to the officer who has been sent to execute him (verses 14-16)? What do you think Daniel might have said? (*Hint:* Jot down a few wise and tactful responses he might have given.)

3. What does Daniel's reaction tell us about how he handled pressure? What do you think fueled his responses?

4. Once he had bought some time, to whom did Daniel turn for help (verses 17-18)? What did he specifically ask them to do?

5. What do we learn from the examples of Daniel and his friends about how to handle difficult situations that take us by surprise?

6. How did God respond to this crisis (verse 19)? What do we learn about God from His response?

7. What did Arioch believe was the solution to the king's problem (verse 25)? Where did Daniel immediately place the focus (verses 27-28)?

8. How did the king respond to Daniel's interpretation (verses 46-47)?

9. How did God bless Daniel for standing firm in his faith under pressure?

10. Do you think God still rewards men for taking steps of faith for Him? When have you experienced or observed this?

Connect with the Group

Group Opener
Discuss the group-opener question and the discussion questions that follow.

How do you usually respond to situations that have a direct negative impact on you but are outside of your control?

Discussion Questions

a. Why do we have a tendency to panic when circumstances catch us off-guard?

b. Consider Daniel's example. What can we learn from him about what to do when we're in panic mode?

c. Do you think God wants us to involve others in our crises? Why or why not? What does involving others in our crises accomplish for us? for them?

d. What can we do to train ourselves to respond in faith rather than react with fear? Based on your own experience, what practical advice could you give others in this regard?

e. When God answers your prayers, provides the wisdom you need, or delivers you from imminent danger, how do you usually respond?

f. Compare your typical response with Daniel's response. (See Daniel 2:20-23.) List one or two insights.

g. What positive spiritual impact might your reactions to unpredictable situations have on those around you?

Standing Strong

Describe a situation in your own life or in the lives of people close to you in which God is giving you an opportunity to trust Him with something big.

Enlist some friends (or members of your men's group) to pray for God's mercy and guidance in this situation. Pray for good outcomes and results that will bring glory to God.

not "on board"

Experiencing Deliverance Through Devotion to God

Key Verses

Shadrach, Meshach and Abednego replied to the king, "O Nebuchadnezzar, we do not need to defend ourselves before you in this matter. If we are thrown into the blazing furnace, the God we serve is able to save us from it, and he will rescue us from your hand, O king. But even if he does not, we want you to know, O king, that we will not serve your gods or worship the image of gold you have set up." (Daniel 3:16-18)

Goals for Growth

- Reject the demands of men if it means sinning against God.
- Remember that God allows trials in my life to reveal His power.
- Allow God to use my trials to reveal Himself to others.

Head Start

No one likes to stand out if it means being ridiculed. So what do we do? We blend in; we go with the flow; we don't rock the boat. Majority opinion prevails most of the time, and democracy has trained us to swallow the results of elections when more than 50 percent of the vote carries.

Thankfully, no one posts our photo on the six o'clock news and announces that we voted against the majority. We aren't branded a dissenter either, and the threat of a political assassination never enters our mind. But Daniel and his three friends faced such perils in Babylon.

That empire was not a democracy; it was a monarchy. Votes were not cast; rather, edicts and decrees flowed from the king's mouth right into the law books. And why not? The king was considered divine and could rule as he wished.

For loyal subjects, life could change on a dime. Noncompliance to the king's edicts meant being branded a dissenter, which resulted in a one-way ticket to the brick furnaces. No questions asked, no two hundred dollars for passing "Go," and certainly no appeals. Once a law was written, it was a done deal. Break the law, feel the pain.

Times may change, but God's man faces trials of courage in every age. Nero blamed the Christians for the Great Fire of Rome in AD 64, and the slaughter that followed would have been a media bonanza. Dietrich Bonhoeffer, a pastor in Hitler's Nazi Germany, stood strongly for Christianity (which didn't blend well with a master-race theology), and he was hanged from the gallows. In China today, being a committed Christian means being branded a counterrevolutionary. Christians constantly risk persecution or imprisonment, or they might even disappear.

Most believers in the Western world may never face this kind of test of their Christian commitment. But that doesn't diminish the temptation to blend in, to not ruffle feathers, to go with the flow—living as God's man, but incognito.

We have ample opportunities in our culture to stand out and stand up for our faith, to go against the grain, and we have thousands of choices in our lifetime to bring praise and glory to our Savior and Redeemer.

The question is, Will we choose to stand out? Or will we just get on board with the crowd and play it safe?

Connect with the Word

Read Daniel 3.

1. What decree did the king issue (verses 1-5)? What did he require? What was the consequence of noncompliance (verse 6)?

2. How did everyone in the kingdom respond (verse 7)?

3. What complaint was lodged against God's men (verse 12)?
   What did their response to the decree get them in return?

4. What was required of Shadrach, Meshach, and Abednego to
   respond the way they did to the decree (verses 16-18)?

5. What was their perspective on the whole situation (verses 17-
   18)? What did they willingly choose rather than bowing down
   to the image of gold?

6. What did their bold stand accomplish in the short term
   (verse 19)?

7. When did God deliver Shadrach, Meshach, and Abednego from
   the fire? What insights does God's timing in this situation give
   you about how He works?

8. What practical encouragement do you find in verse 25?

9. What would Nebuchadnezzar have missed if Shadrach, Meshach, and Abednego had not taken a stand for God? (That is, what did he see as a result of their stand that he wouldn't have seen otherwise?)

Connect with the Group

Group Opener
Read the group opener aloud and discuss the questions that follow.

When I (Kenny) first became a Christian, I didn't care about what people thought of my faith in Christ. I was so stoked to be going to heaven that I couldn't understand why anyone wouldn't want to get to know about Jesus for himself. I was so gung-ho about sharing my faith that I even practiced in front of my bathroom mirror. Once I gave it a shot, however, the rejections started coming. Friends dropped off. People mocked me behind my back. Others told me to get lost; they weren't interested.

I went from being the life of the party to the social outcast. I recall being at a school friend's house one Saturday night, and some of them were drinking in the back. When a girl in my class had too much to drink, I volunteered to give her a ride home, but then a buddy on my basketball team leaned into the car and said, "Is she going to come back born again?" Then he and all his buddies had a good laugh at my spiritual ego's expense.

I felt so rejected that night. In fact, incidents like that caused me to question my self-worth. Other doubts crept in, which caused me to fear what other people thought of me. I can remember fudging or doing little things to misrepresent myself, all to gain the approval of my friends. If friends asked me how my college plans were coming or, later, when supervisors asked how a project was going at work, I would puff the situation up to make it seem better than it really was.

Worse, when I was outnumbered or verbally outgunned, I learned how to deflect discussions away from my faith. I did anything to stave off the possibility of rejection. I craved approval, not knowing at the time that my behavior was preventing me from really growing as God's man.

The price I paid was in my own heart and character. Every time I played to people, I stunted my Christian growth. To this day, it amazes me how much influence people had over my actions. Should I make the business situation at work look great, or admit that the deal was going south? Should I join in a conversation slamming someone, or should I stand up for that person and encourage my friends not to talk about him in that way? Should I step through the door God has opened and tell the story of how Christ changed my life, or should I mumble something about, "Wow, thanks for telling me that"?

Once when I was teaching a class on sharing your faith, I said, "Raise your hand if fear of rejection is your number one reason for not sharing your faith." Of the eighty men in that class, nearly everyone raised his hand. Why? Our hearts are divided. We have no spines. We end up playing to the crowd.

Yet God never intended for us to live in that kind of fear for this simple reason: *God's man lives for an audience of One.*

> Fear of man will prove to be a snare, but whoever trusts in the LORD is kept safe. Many seek an audience with a ruler, but it is from the LORD that man gets justice. (Proverbs 29:25-26)

Fact time: If God alone measures our lives, we are free to live for God without apology or reservation. That's when we feel most like Jesus.[2]

Discussion Questions

a. What do you think of the statement, "Every time I played to people, I stunted my Christian growth"? What is your experience with this?

---

2. Arterburn and Luck, *Every Man, God's Man,* 27-29.

b. What action steps can you glean from the Proverbs passage that will help you take a fearless stand for God?

c. What lifestyle challenges does God's man face in today's culture? Name some specific examples.

d. What situations tend to test your loyalty to Christ the most?

e. Why do you think God places us in situations that test our loyalty to Him?

f. What gives God's man the kind of confidence that stares death in the face and the kind of hope expressed by Daniel's buddies? (See Daniel 3:16-18.)

g. When have you been in the furnace most recently? Did you sense God's presence amidst this fiery trial—or not? What happened?

h. In your opinion, what does God want us to know when we are feeling the heat of a trial? (Check out Isaiah 43:1-2.)

Standing Strong

What practical actions can you take this week in the following areas:

Trusting God in the face of opposition:

Defying the culture when it opposes God's ways:

Sacrificing for the kingdom, even when it's difficult:

Refusing to get "on board," even when it means disappointing others:

not pulling punches

Speaking What People Need to Hear in the Moment

Key Verse

Therefore, O king, be pleased to accept my advice: Renounce your sins by doing what is right, and your wickedness by being kind to the oppressed. It may be that then your prosperity will continue. (Daniel 4:27)

Goals for Growth

- Use the wisdom God gives me to help others.
- Faithfully speak the truth in love.
- Trust God to take my words and use them in His time.

Head Start

Having counseled men in the area of sexual sin over the years, I (Kenny) have firmly concluded that when a man deceives himself into sexual disobedience, the only way to snap him out of it is to throw a right cross to the jaw (metaphorically speaking, of course).

It does no good to dance around the issues. The only way to address them is to zero in on the facts about his wrongdoing and talk about the present and future consequences of his actions—the miseries on earth and on Judgment Day. He's made the biggest mistake (in my opinion) that a man can make as a husband and a father. He's been blinded by the adrenaline of sexual desire. He's been fogged in by the temporary mood elevation of escaping responsibility. He has failed to slay the dragon of self-deception.

So whether I'm meeting with a man who is seeking help for himself or trying to help a brother avoid a sexual train wreck, I find that my sensitivity training must yield to a shock-treatment approach. Even then, many men don't listen. They choose their own destructive path. And they keep walking that path until the level of pain they experience exceeds the pain of making things right.

As an adviser, Daniel knew this dilemma well. The only difference is that his counselee was a king with spiritual amnesia. Nebuchadnezzar just didn't seem to remember the landmark moments when God was trying to get his attention. Pride, a pagan culture, and an ample supply of yes-men can do this to a king. Yet when he finally came to his senses and went to the one man who had heavenly insight, Nebuchadnezzar couldn't seem to put on the brakes and stop his pride from ruining him.

Fortunately for King Nebuchadnezzar, Daniel was always a straight shooter and, in this respect, the most loyal of servants. He never sugarcoated the messages God gave him. He knew nothing of spin. He pulled no punches. He knew only to pass on the truth in the ways God told him. And in the process, he showed all God's men how to administer the truth.

Connect with the Word

Read Daniel 4.

1. Be Daniel for a moment. Why are you so unsettled by King Nebuchadnezzar's dream (verse 19)?

2. What did the dream portend for the king?

3. Why did God have to severely prune the king? What outcome was assured if Nebuchadnezzar obeyed Daniel's advice (verse 26)?

4. What main action steps did Daniel advise the king to take (verse 27)?

5. What did Nebuchadnezzar do in spite of Daniel's advice (verses 28-30)?

6. What was God's response to the king's "I'm God" speech (verses 31-33)?

7. What brought the king's wilderness experience to an end (verses 34-36)?

8. What connection do you see between Daniel's advice in verse 27 and the king's prayer in verses 34-37?

9. What did God want Nebuchadnezzar to realize as a result of his wilderness experience and Daniel's willingness to boldly speak God's Word to him (verse 37)?

Connect with the Group

Group Opener

Discuss the group-opener question and the discussion questions that follow.

Is there a "Daniel" in your life who isn't afraid to tell you what you need to hear rather than what you want to hear? What impact has this person had on your life?

Discussion Questions

a. Why do we need other men to help us grow?

b. What role have other men played in God's pruning process in your life?

c. What is God's goal when He uses someone to confront your pride? If you can, indicate a passage in the New Testament that supports your response.

d. What differences do you see between Daniel's obedience and the king's?

e. What are the benefits of surrendering to God's authority and leadership? (See Daniel 4:34-37.)

f. What should be our motive when we offer advice to a brother? What should be our ultimate goal?

g. In your opinion, what should a man do if a brother refuses to accept godly advice? What is the next step to take with this brother? (See Matthew 18:15-17.)

Standing Strong

List the people in your life with whom God has given you significant influence.

Read both Ephesians 4:25,29 and Proverbs 27:5-6. Pray about your role in the lives of those you listed above (such as encourager, listener, accountability partner, etc.). Ask God to use you to help them become better worshipers and followers of Jesus Christ.

not afraid to do a hard thing

Being Obedient in Tough Circumstances

Key Verses

This is what these words mean: *Mene:* God has numbered the days of your reign and brought it to an end. *Tekel:* You have been weighed on the scales and found wanting. *Peres:* Your kingdom is divided and given to the Medes and Persians. (Daniel 5:26-28)

Goals for Growth

- Push past feelings to obedience.
- Complete the work God has given me to do in spite of difficulties.
- Trust in God's sovereignty over tough circumstances.

Head Start

The toughest moments in my (Kenny's) years as a CEO? Firing employees or laying them off. I hated everything about it. Both situations meant uncomfortable meetings, tears, exit interviews, more tears, family issues, health-insurance coverage, and severance-package negotiations.

Did I mention tears?

Hovering over it all, of course, was the pain of looking a guy in the face and giving him the worst news of his year. I can even remember having to do this around Christmastime on a few occasions. As bad as I felt about what I had to do and as much as I hated doing it, I always believed it was the right thing for our company. I had to trust that God would take care of people.

So even across these many centuries, I can relate to Daniel. The next king of Babylon had no use for Daniel, who was about eighty years old at the time. He called on Daniel only to satisfy his curiosity, not to get advice. This new king also hadn't learned from his daddy's failings—it seems arrogance ran in the family. Like his father, Belshazzar would reap the consequences for getting drunk on pride and slinging it in God's face.

Yet God had had enough. In the midst of a royal Babylonian rave party, He shocked hosts and guests alike with a mysterious handwritten wall engraving that seemed to appear out of nowhere. (People now use the famous phrase "the handwriting is on the wall" to describe some imminent doom.)

As usual, none of the regular wise men had what it took to interpret the writing on the wall, which totally spooked the king. But the queen intervened, reminding Belshazzar of a man who had the ability to interpret dreams and explain riddles. So Daniel was brought in to handle a job no one else could tackle. He immediately knew what the writing said, though he still had to endure the shallow flattery of a king whose party had just crashed. This had to be superuncomfortable. But in the mind of God's man, there was no turning back.

Sometimes God selects us to do what only we can do in order to allow Him to do what only He can do. It doesn't always feel good. But will we push past our feelings? Will we be obedient in tough situations and trust God with the outcome?

Connect with the Word

Read Daniel 5.

1. What do verses 1-4 suggest about Belshazzar's character?

2. Why do you think God picked this time to communicate His judgment to the king? Why do you think God chose to write on the wall?

3. Why did God involve Daniel? What purpose did that serve?

4. Be Daniel for a moment. What is going through your mind on the way to the palace?

5. How did Daniel handle the situation when he arrived (verses 13-17)? How did he respond to the king's flattery (verse 17)?

6. What did Daniel do in verses 18-21? If you had been Daniel, would this speech have been difficult or easy for you? Explain.

7. What message was God communicating to the king through Daniel in verses 22 and 23? How did Daniel know these details? Why do you think God had him go into this detail?

8. What was God measuring on His scales (verse 27)? (*Suggestion:* Verses 22 and 23 may be helpful in answering this question.)

9. Whose responsibility was it to remove the proud king from power?

Connect with the Group

Group Opener

Read the group opener aloud and discuss the questions that follow.

I (Kenny) was a new Christian when I began attending UCLA, and I still remember feeling confused when I heard people praying for humility. How would you know when your prayers were answered? Were you supposed to simply act humbly? Refuse compliments? Dress in a plain white shirt and black slacks? Never call attention to yourself? As I pondered these questions, it seemed to me that people trying to be humble (like me) were ending up taking pride in the fact that they were more humble than others, which defeated the whole purpose of acting humbly in the first place!

Ironically, I got my first working definition of humility by watching a football movie called *Rudy*. This film, based on a true story, is about a steel-town kid who dreams big—Notre Dame big—in his personal David-and-Goliath quest. Not only is pint-sized Rudy Ruettiger too small and slow to be an outside linebacker, he also doesn't have the grades to get into Notre Dame. Nor does he come from the right side of town. But Rudy never gives up in the face of overwhelming odds. Against conventional wisdom and the advice of his family and even his fiancée, Rudy packs his bags, lands a custodial job at Notre Dame stadium, and enrolls in a South Bend junior college. Rudy is so close he can taste his dream coming true.

In the process, Rudy is encouraged by a local priest (Father Cavanaugh) who mentors and helps him persevere in spite of one rejection letter after another. After his third rejection, Rudy is battling despair—but praying—when Father Cavanaugh bumps into him.

FC: Taking your appeal to a Higher Authority?

Rudy: I am desperate. If I don't get in next semester, I am over. Done. Notre Dame doesn't accept senior transfers.

FC: Well, you've done a helluva job, lad, chasing your dream.

Rudy: I don't care what kind of a job I did. If it doesn't produce results, it doesn't mean anything.

FC: I think you'll discover that it will.

Rudy: Maybe I haven't prayed enough.

FC: I don't think that's your problem. Praying is something we do on our time. The answers come in God's time.

Rudy: Have I done everything I can? Will you help me?

FC: Son, in thirty-five years of religious studies, I've come up with only two incontrovertible facts: There is a God, and I am not Him.[3]

Discussion Questions

a. Have you ever pursued a dream with the perseverance of a Rudy? Talk about it.

b. In what ways is Rudy an example of true humility?

3. Arterburn and Luck, *Every Man, God's Man*, 121-22.

c. What is your reaction to the statement, "There is a God, and I am not Him"? When have you been most aware of this truth in your life?

d. Why does God seem to take extreme measures to deal with prideful men?

e. In light of Belshazzar's mistake, what mistakes from your own family of origin do you not want to repeat? What can you do to keep history from repeating itself?

f. Why is it important to have people around us who are able to help us keep our pride in check?

g. How does knowing that God measures a man on the scales of pride and humility affect how you view yourself and your walk with God?

h. In what areas of your life do you think you might be found wanting in God's eyes? Talk about it.

i. Look again at Daniel 5:22-23. What can God's man learn from Belshazzar's failures about how to live before God?

Standing Strong

Do you know someone with whom you need to have a tough conversation? Do you need to confront a sin in that person's life, or are you aware of an attitude that, if unchecked, will lead to God's judgment? What steps will you take to address the problem in love?

Write a prayer expressing to God what you would like Him to find when your life is measured in the last days. (See 2 Corinthians 5:10.)

not intimidated

Living for an Audience of One

Key Verse

Then they said to the king, "Daniel, who is one of the exiles from Judah, pays no attention to you, O king, or to the decree you put in writing. He still prays three times a day." (Daniel 6:13)

Goals for Growth

- Become more concerned about what God thinks than about what other people think.
- Be bold in the face of intimidation.
- Be willing to pay the price of commitment.

Head Start

Before you're invited to join a college fraternity, you go through a week-long process known as "rush week." I (Kenny) had a blast visiting the different groups of guys to see which fraternity seemed the best fit for all concerned. I played sports and more sports with a great bunch of athletes. From my perspective, there was nothing not to like about frat life.

But a couple details complicated things: I *wasn't* a big drinker and I *was* a Christian. (This was a big change for me, by the way. Just a year earlier I would have been first in line at the keg, quoting "eat, drink, and be merry" from the Bible.) The fact that I was a little different bugged a lot of the older frat guys because drinking alcohol was so central to their idea of "fraternity." But the expectation that I would be the next star of the fraternity basketball team helped them overlook my two glaring character flaws, and I joined.

I didn't realize the pressure cooker I was stepping into. Every weekend during football season our house would rent buses to take everyone to the games at the Rose Bowl. Babes and beer. *Lots* of beer.

While almost everyone was partaking, I sat in the back of the bus hoping I wouldn't be singled out for a guzzling demonstration— but I was. All eyes turned to me, the Christian pledge, and the pressure was on. I smiled and said, "No thanks." One of the older guys then came out with, "What a pussy!" (as in "pussycat"), and the focus moved to the next willing pledge. But my embarrassment hung in the air.

Then a great thought came to me: *If that guy's opinion mattered, then I'd care. But since it doesn't, I don't. What matters is what God thinks.*

Guys are always trying to fit in, and they do the weirdest things to gain the approval of other men. But when you are God's man, you're doing more than just compromising a standard when you give in to intimidation; you're denying your faith and Christ.

The turning point for me in this battle with approval addiction is the Cross. When I gaze long and hard at the blood-spilling commitment of my Savior, pleasing men means nothing to me. No one else will ever come close to expressing that much love, sacrifice, courage, and commitment—for me!

Jesus's commitment to us makes our decisions a lot easier when we filter our choices in light of the huge choice He made that dark and gloomy Friday afternoon in Jerusalem. I can't dishonor His sacrifice.

Daniel must have reached a similar conclusion. We know he refused to be intimidated and play to people at the expense of his faith. Period. Even when the lions bared their fangs.

What a different world this would be if all God's men, with unbending commitment, refused to cave in and compromise!

Connect with the Word

Read Daniel 6.

1. What qualities made Daniel different from the other government administrators (verses 3-4)?

2. What was the response of Daniel's co-workers in verse 5? What do their comments tell us about who Daniel really was?

3. What dilemma did Daniel face (verses 6-9)? How did he respond to the challenge (verse 10)?

4. Why did Daniel seemingly have such an easy time deciding what to do in response to the king's decree? What does that tell us about his relationship with God?

5. According to verses 10 and 11, what was the substance of Daniel's prayers?

6. In such a perilous situation, did thanking God make sense? Explain. (*Suggestion:* Recall a situation in your life when thanking God was the best response.)

7. What evidence did Daniel's adversaries use to indict him
   (verse 13)?

8. What price was Daniel willing to pay for his faithfulness
   to God?

9. How does the situation look to you in verse 17? What saved
   Daniel in the end (verses 22-23)?

10. What was the end result of Daniel's decision to fear God more
    than he feared men (verses 26,28)? What personal application
    comes to mind?

Connect with the Group

Group Opener
Discuss the group-opener question and the discussion questions that follow.

What situations often cause men to retreat from their convictions? What are the most intimidating situations for you personally in this regard?

Discussion Questions

a. What's your reputation at work? How do you want people to think of you?

b. Why does God put us in pressure-cooker situations? (That is, what qualities do we develop when we consistently choose to obey God under pressure?)

c. What makes it easier for you to choose God when you're under pressure?

d. What role does prayer play in the battle against the temptation to compromise? What do you glean from Daniel's prayers that can help you in your own battle?

e. If people wanted to build a case against you as a committed believer, would they find enough evidence to destroy your reputation? Explain.

f. What does Daniel's story in this chapter reveal about God's timing? What do you think determines when God will intervene in a crisis we're going through?

g. Based on Daniel 6, what impact might our radical stand for God have on those who observe us?

h. Does God want to bless our obedience? How do you know?

Standing Strong

In which areas of your life do you need to develop a greater ability to resist intimidation and remain faithful to God?

Complete the following prayer:

Lord, I would like to be known as a man who. . .

not making excuses

Choosing Responsibility over Blame

Key Verses

O Lord, the great and awesome God, who keeps his covenant of love with all who love him and obey his commands, we have sinned and done wrong. We have been wicked and have rebelled; we have turned away from your commands and laws. (Daniel 9:4-5)

Goals for Growth

- Eliminate the habit of blaming others.
- Energetically pursue repentance and confession when needed.
- Immediately apply God's revealed truth to my words and deeds.

Head Start

Corner a man with the truth, and you'll quickly see what he's made of. When we get pinned down under a heavy accusation, we usually come out with guns blazing.

The fact is, no man likes to own the worst parts of his life. It's shameful and it's emotionally burdensome. That's why many of us have developed sensors that detect criticism coming a mile away. Then we run for the hills, so to speak. We may not be able to leave the room, but we can manipulate and spin the conversation. We may not be able to shake the blame, but we can make sure others share it so we won't look like the exclusive source of the trouble. We may deny the rap, but we can't deny the truth inside.

There's a flip side to this coin, though. Imagine you're the guy who's keeping his side of the street clean. You're living right, not breaking any laws. You're winning friends and influencing people. Your entire life is dedicated to helping people by giving counsel that improves their lives. You speak the truth. You stand up for God. You have like-minded friends who believe in you. You are a shining example of what's best about your faith and country. You are Daniel.

Now imagine that a great disaster has fallen upon you because of the sins and shortcomings of your own countrymen. You and many other innocent bystanders are unjustly forced into captivity. So now you have to make a decision: Am I going to get bitter and complain that the failings of others brought all this misery on me? Or am I going to get busy spiritually and offer practical help?

Daniel was an amazing dude. He didn't believe that bitterness served God's man or God's purposes. He didn't believe in making excuses or blaming others. But he did believe in helping in whatever specific and unique ways he could.

When you have every right to be bitter but choose instead to help the very people who brought disaster to your front porch, that's real character!

Connect with the Word

Read Daniel 9:1-19.

1. According to verse 2, what specifically did Daniel glean from the Scriptures?

2. What actions do you think Daniel was motivated to take after seeing God's plan for the future?

3. What did Daniel do in response to the alarming news (verse 3)?

4. In light of verse 3, how would you describe Daniel's prayer life?

5. Why do you think Daniel made no distinction between his own sins and the sins of his people (verses 7-9)?

6. What happens when we thumb our noses at God's commands and reject the advice of people who tell us the truth (verse 11)? Have you ever experienced this personally? Care to tell about it?

7. Based on verse 13, how would you define *repentance*?

8. What would it mean for the people to give attention to God's truth?

9. Why do you think Daniel chose to put himself in the same boat as the rest of the people?

Connect with the Group

Group Opener
Read the group opener aloud and discuss the questions that follow.

Jack always knew that his friend Alex would inquire how he was doing. But on this occasion, Jack hoped his Christian buddy wouldn't show for their Friday morning breaktime coffee. The previous night, Jack had typed the key words *adult entertainment* into his search engine, and by the time he finished clicking through several hundred Web pages three hours later, he felt dirty and far from God.

Jack wished he could say something...get some help...but Alex was a church elder, and if he learned that Jack was hooked on Internet porn, Jack would be called before an emergency meeting of the elder board—after which he would have to perform public penance of some sort. Jack couldn't face that, so he kept his mouth shut.

Nice cover-up, Pastor Jack.

The first cousin of honesty for God's man is confession. For the most part, we men are not good at it. We choke on phrases like:

- "I was wrong."
- "I am sorry."
- "You are right."
- "I need to ask your forgiveness."

We are cowards. We just don't have the stomach for confession because it forces us to confront our actions and ourselves. No one likes to do that. Revealing our personal hang-ups or issues is too risky, so it's better to lie low. But the alternative is much worse.

- We lose intimacy with God.
- We lose intimacy with our wives.
- We lose intimacy with our kids.
- We lose credibility with others.
- We lose connection with the truth.
- We lose fellowship with the Holy Spirit.
- We lose something from our character.
- We lose days, weeks, months, even years of joy and peace.[4]

Discussion Questions

a. If you were counseling Pastor Jack, what advice would you give him?

b. Do you agree that some form of "public penance" would be required if Jack decided to come clean with Alex? Why or why not?

---

4. Arterburn and Luck, *Every Man, God's Man*, 152-53.

c. At what levels, if any, can you relate to this scene from Jack's life? Do you find it difficult or easy to share with the other guys where Jack's story intersects with your own? Explain.

d. What is the number one excuse men give for not regularly being in God's Word? What do excuses reveal about us?

e. How does a lack of confession cause a lack of intimacy in our relationships?

f. Daniel turned to the Lord first when faced with a crisis. To whom or what do we turn instead of God?

g. When we blow it, how can we find our way back to a fully restored connection with God? What does it involve? (See Daniel 9:13.)

h. What sin(s) do you need to turn from today? Or what truth do you need to give attention to (stop ignoring)?

Standing Strong

Whom do you tend to blame for some of the problems you face? Write their names here.

What responsibilities do you avoid accepting? List them here.

Write a prayer to God expressing your desire to accept responsibility for the changes you need to make in your life.

not careless with God's plan

Staying Sharp Through the Spiritual Discipline of Prayer

Key Verse

Since the first day that you set your mind to gain understanding and to humble yourself before your God, your words were heard, and I have come in response to them. (Daniel 10:12)

Goals for Growth

- Consistently turn to God for understanding.
- Develop persistence in prayer.
- Willingly receive encouragement and strength from God.

Head Start

As chaplain of a cancer unit, I (Kenny) felt as if I'd earned a master's degree in bad news. For an entire year my life centered around brain tumors, biopsies, lumpectomies, chemotherapies, radiation, support groups, family meetings, eulogies, tears, and hugs—lots of hugs.

The "C" word for many of us is a death sentence, and its emotional impact is titanic. As a chaplain I watched people melt down right in front of me. I witnessed husbands break down like little boys who had lost their mommies. But they were grown men losing their wives. Everything they knew was changing forever.

What amazed me were the varied responses to the disease, which ranged from dark bitterness to resigned fatalism to optimistic faith. The most encouraging patients were the diligent ones who faced this battle with pit-bull determination. They weren't careless about their future. They weren't going to lie down and accept their fate. They were determined to fight their disease by learning all they could, doing all they could, and accepting all the help they could. And many of them were committed to believing all they could in God's sovereign and watchful care over their lives. Cancer's grip on their future motivated them to live with purpose, intention, and most amazingly, thankfulness.

Daniel experienced a disturbing encounter with his future when he was broadsided with a revelation, a news bulletin concerning a great war that was to come. The vision was so disturbing that he said, "I am overcome with anguish because of the vision, my lord, and I am helpless. How can I, your servant, talk with you, my lord? My strength is gone and I can hardly breathe" (Daniel 10:16-17).

Daniel was a man, just like you and me, who could be rocked and destabilized by crisis, yet he turned to the Rock to find security and purpose amid the storm. Knowing that God's hand was on his future made him careful to pursue God's purpose and presence with great diligence. He wanted to handle the situation the right way, which meant "dialing in" all of his spiritual resources.

The prognosis may have been bad, but the journey was amazing because Daniel didn't give in to doubt or fear. He wasn't careless. Instead he gave himself entirely over to God's plan.

Connect with the Word

Read Daniel 10.

1. How did Daniel react to the news bulletin from God (verses 2-3)? Why do you think he reacted this way?

2. What do you think is the connection between Daniel's persistence in prayer and his encounter with the messenger "dressed in linen" (verse 5)?

3. Why do you think Daniel saw this man and others didn't?

4. What were the keys to Daniel's special connection to God's network of help as described by the messenger (verses 12-13)?

5. What do we learn about God from the messenger's words to Daniel in verse 12? What is He looking for in us?

6. When did God hear Daniel's prayer? When did help arrive? Why the delay?

7. What does this passage tell us about our spiritual battle?

8. What did God want Daniel to know (verses 11,19)?

9. What happens when we are able to hear and receive God's encouragement (verse 19)?

Connect with the Group

Group Opener
Discuss the group-opener question and the discussion questions that follow.

What impact does knowing that God is personally for you, His adopted son, have on the way you view Him? yourself?

Discussion Questions
a. When the future looks bleak, how do you typically react?

b. What do you do to "dial in" God's presence during your day?

c. What is your definition of prayer? How would you describe the connection between prayer and being aware of God's presence?

d. In what areas besides food could you practice disciplining your appetites in order to hear and see God more clearly in your life? Do you find it difficult or easy to discipline yourself in these areas? Talk about it.

e. Why is it good to say no to yourself while you are saying yes to God?

f. In what ways are men careless with God's purposes for their lives?

g. Why do you think many men don't experience God's personal presence and touch in the ways Daniel did? Do you believe God still desires to communicate intimately with us today? Explain.

h. How do you humble yourself before the Lord?

i. What can a man do to develop greater persistence and diligence in seeking God's will through prayer? What will it take?

j. Imagine having a more focused and rich prayer life. What might be some of the effects in your life?

Standing Strong

List the obstacles you believe are keeping you from having a more disciplined prayer life. Which obstacles can you eliminate? How?

Write down some of the ways you'd like your experience with God to become more personal and meaningful. Open your heart to God in prayer and let Him know your desires. Ask Him to reveal Himself more personally to you in the days to come.

small-group resources

leader tips

What if men aren't doing the Connect with the Word section before our small-group session?

Don't be discouraged. You set the pace. If you are doing the study and regularly referring to it in conversations with your men throughout the week, they will pick up on its importance. Here are some suggestions to motivate the men in your group to do their home Bible study:

- Send out a midweek e-mail in which you share your answer to one of the study questions. This shows them that you are personally committed to and involved in the study.
- Ask the guys to hit "respond to all" on their e-mail program and share one insight from that week's Bible study with the entire group. Encourage them to send it out before the next small-group session.
- Every time you meet, ask each man in the group to share one insight from his home study.

What if men are not showing up for small group?

This might mean they are losing a sin battle and don't want to admit it to the group. Or they might be consumed with other priorities. Or maybe they don't think they're getting anything out of the group. Here are some suggestions for getting the guys back each week:

- Affirm them when they show up, and tell them how much it means to you that they make small group a priority.

- From time to time, ask them to share one reason small group is important to them.
- Regularly call or send out an e-mail the day before you meet to remind them you're looking forward to seeing them.
- Check in with any guy who has missed more than one session and find out what's going on in his life.
- Get some feedback from the men. You may need to adjust your style. Listen and learn.

What if group discussion is not happening?

You are a discussion facilitator. You have to keep guys involved in the discussion or you'll lose them. You can engage a man who isn't sharing by saying, "Chuck, you've been quiet. What do you think about this question or discussion?" You should also be prepared to share your own personal stories that are related to the discussion questions. You'll set the example by the kind of sharing you do.

What if one man is dominating the group time?

You have to deal with it. If you don't, men will stop showing up. No one wants to hear from just one guy all the time. It will quickly kill morale. Meet with the guy in person and privately. Firmly but gently suggest that he allow others more time to talk. Be positive and encouraging, but truthful. You might say, "Bob, I notice how enthusiastic you are about the group and how you're always prepared to share your thoughts with the group. But there are some pretty quiet guys in the group too. Have you noticed? Would you be willing to help me get them involved in speaking up?"

How do I get the guys in my group more involved?

Give them something to do. Ask one guy to bring a snack. Invite another to lead the prayer time (ask in advance). Have a guy sub for you one week as the leader. (Meet with him beforehand to walk through the group program and the time allotments for each segment.) Encourage another guy to lead a subgroup.

What if guys are not being vulnerable during the Standing Strong or prayer times?

You model openness. You set the pace. Honesty breeds honesty. Vulnerability breeds vulnerability. Are you being vulnerable and honest about your own problems and struggles? (This doesn't mean that you have to spill your guts each week or reveal every secret of your life.) Remember, men want an honest, on-their-level leader who strives to walk with God. (Also, as the leader, you need an accountability partner, perhaps another group leader.)

What will we do at the first session?

We encourage you to open by discussing the **Small-Group Covenant** we've included in this resource section. Ask the men to commit to the study, and then discuss how long it will take your group to complete each session. (We suggest 75-90 minute sessions.) Men find it harder to come up with excuses for missing a group session if they have made a covenant to the other men right at the start.

Begin to identify ways certain men can play a more active role in small group. Give away responsibility. You won't feel as burdened, and your men will grow from the experience. Keep in mind that this process can take a few weeks. Challenge men to fulfill one of the group roles identified later in this resource section. If no one steps forward to fill a role, say to one of the men, "George, I've noticed that you are comfortable praying in a group. Would you lead us each week during that time?"

How can we keep the group connected after we finish a study?

Begin talking about starting another Bible study before you finish this eight-week study. (There are several other studies to choose from in the Every Man Bible study series.) Consider having a social time at the conclusion of the study, and encourage the men to invite a friend. This will help create momentum and encourage growth as you launch into another study with your group. There are probably many men in your church or neighborhood who aren't in small groups but would like to be. Be the kind of group that includes others.

As your group grows, consider choosing an apprentice leader who can take half the group into another room for the **Connect with the Group** time. That subgroup can stay together for prayer, or you can reconvene as a large group during that time. You could also meet for discussion as a large group and then break into subgroups for **Standing Strong** and **prayer.**

If your group doubles in size, it might be a perfect opportunity to release your apprentice leader with half the group to start another group. Allow men to pray about this and make a decision as a group. Typically, the relational complexities that come into play when a small group births a new group work themselves out. Allow guys to choose which group they'd like to be a part of. If guys are slow in choosing one group or another, ask them individually to select one of the groups. Take the lead in making this happen.

Look for opportunities for your group to serve in the church or community. Consider a local outreach project or a short-term missions trip. There are literally hundreds of practical ways you can serve the Lord in outreach. Check with your church leaders to learn the needs in your congregation or community. Create some interest by sending out scouts who will return with a report for the group. Serving keeps men from becoming self-focused and ingrown. When you serve as a group, you will grow as a group.

using this study in a large-group format

Many church leaders are looking for biblically based curriculum that can be used in a large-group setting, such as a Sunday-school class, or for small groups within an existing larger men's group. Each of the Every Man Bible studies can be adapted for this purpose. In addition, this curriculum can become a catalyst for churches wishing to launch men's small groups or to build a men's ministry.

Getting Started

Begin by getting the word out to men in your church, inviting them to join you for a men's study based on one of the topics in the Every Man Bible study series. You can place a notice in your church bulletin, have the pastor announce it from the pulpit, or pursue some other means of attracting interest.

Orientation Week

Arrange your room with round tables and chairs. Put approximately six chairs at each table.

Start your session in prayer and introduce your topic with a short but motivational message from any of the scriptures used in the Bible study. Hand out the curriculum and challenge the men to do their homework before each session. During this first session give the men some discussion questions based upon an overview of the material and have them talk things through within their small group around the table.

Just before you wrap things up, have each group select a table host or leader. You can do this by having everyone point at once to the person at their table they feel would best facilitate discussion for future meetings.

Ask those newly elected table leaders to stay after for a few minutes, and offer them an opportunity to be further trained as small-group leaders as they lead discussions throughout the course of the study.

Subsequent Weeks

Begin in prayer. Then give a short message (15-25 minutes) based upon the scripture used for that lesson. Pull out the most motivating topics or points, and strive to make the discussion relevant to the everyday life and world of a typical man. Then leave time for each table to work through the discussion questions listed in the curriculum. Be sure the discussion facilitators at each table close in prayer.

At the end of the eight sessions, you might want to challenge each "table group" to become a small group, inviting them to meet regularly with their new small-group leader and continue building the relationships they've begun.

prayer request record

Date:

Name:

Prayer Request:

Praise:

Date:

Name:

Prayer Request:

Praise:

Date:

Name:

Prayer Request:

Praise:

Date:

Name:

Prayer Request:

Praise:

Date:

Name:

Prayer Request:

Praise:

defining group roles

Group Leader: Leads the lesson and facilitates group discussion.

Apprentice Leader: Assists the leader as needed, which may include leading the lesson.

Refreshment Coordinator: Maintains a list of who will provide refreshments. Calls group members on the list to remind them to bring what they signed up for.

Prayer Warrior: Serves as the contact person for prayer between sessions. Establishes a list of those willing to pray for needs that arise. Maintains the prayer-chain list and activates the chain as needed by calling the first person on the list.

Social Chairman: Plans any desired social events during group sessions or at another scheduled time. Gathers members for planning committees as needed.

small-group roster

Name:
Address:
Phone: E-mail:

Name:
Address:
Phone: E-mail:

Name:
Address:
Phone: E-mail:

Name:
Address:
Phone: E-mail:

Name:
Address:
Phone: E-mail:

Name:
Address:
Phone: E-mail:

spiritual checkup

Your answers to the statements below will help you determine which areas you need to work on in order to grow spiritually. Mark the appropriate letter to the left of each statement. Then make a plan to take one step toward further growth in each area. Don't forget to pray for the Lord's wisdom before you begin. Be honest. Don't be overly critical or rationalize your weaknesses.

Y = Yes
S = Somewhat or Sometimes
N = No

My Spiritual Connection with Other Believers

____ I am developing relationships with Christian friends.

____ I have joined a small group.

____ I am dealing with conflict in a biblical manner.

____ I have become more loving and forgiving than I was a year ago.

____ I am a loving and devoted husband and father.

My Spiritual Growth

____ I have committed to daily Bible reading and prayer.

____ I am journaling on a regular basis, recording my spiritual growth.

____ I am growing spiritually by studying the Bible with others.

____ I am honoring God in my finances and personal giving.

____ I am filled with joy and gratitude for my life, even during trials.

____ I respond to challenges with peace and faith instead of anxiety and anger.

____ I avoid addictive behaviors (excessive drinking, overeating, watching too much TV, etc.).

Serving Christ and Others

____ I am in the process of discovering my spiritual gifts and talents.

____ I am involved in ministry in my church.

____ I have taken on a role or responsibility in my small group.

____ I am committed to helping someone else grow in his spiritual walk.

Sharing Christ with Others

____ I care about and am praying for those around me who are unbelievers.

____ I share my experience of coming to know Christ with others.

____ I invite others to join me in this group or for weekend worship services.

____ I am praying for others to come to Christ and am seeing this happen.

____ I do what I can to show kindness to people who don't know Christ.

Surrendering My Life for Growth

____ I attend church services weekly.

____ I pray for others to know Christ, and I seek to fulfill the Great Commission.

____ I regularly worship God through prayer, praise, and music, both at church and at home.

____ I care for my body through exercise, nutrition, and rest.

____ I am concerned about using my energy to serve God's purposes instead of my own.

My Identity in the Lord

____ I see myself as a beloved son of God, one whom God loves regardless of my sin.

____ I can come to God in all of my humanity and know that He accepts me completely. When I fail, I willingly run to God for forgiveness.

____ I experience Jesus as an encouraging Friend and Lord each moment of the day.

____ I have an abiding sense that God is on my side. I am aware of His gracious presence with me throughout the day.

____ During moments of beauty, grace, and human connection, I lift up praise and thanks to God.

____ I believe that using my talents to their fullest pleases the Lord.

____ I experience God's love for me in powerful ways.

small-group covenant

As a committed group member, I agree to the following:*

- **Regular Attendance.** I will attend group sessions on time and let everyone know in advance if I can't make it.
- **Group Safety.** I will help create a safe, encouraging environment where men can share their thoughts and feelings without fear of embarrassment or rejection. I will not judge other guys or attempt to fix their problems.
- **Confidentiality.** I will always keep to myself everything that is shared in the group.
- **Acceptance.** I will respect different opinions or beliefs and let Scripture be the teacher.
- **Accountability.** I will make myself accountable to the other group members for the personal goals I share.
- **Friendliness.** I will look for those around me who might join the group and explore their faith with other men.
- **Ownership.** I will prayerfully consider taking on a specific role within the group as the opportunity arises.
- **Spiritual Growth.** I will commit to establishing a daily quiet time with God, which includes doing the homework for this study. I will share with the group the progress I make and the struggles I experience as I seek to grow spiritually.

Signed: _____ Date: _____

---

* *Permission is given to photocopy and distribute this form to each man in your group. Review this covenant quarterly or as needed.*

about the authors

STEPHEN ARTERBURN is coauthor of the best-selling Every Man series. He is also founder and chairman of New Life Clinics, host of the daily *New Life Live!* national radio program, and creator of the Women of Faith conferences. A nationally known speaker and licensed minister, Stephen has authored more than forty books. He lives with his family in Laguna Beach, California.

KENNY LUCK is president and founder of Every Man Ministries, coauthor of *Every Man, God's Man* and its companion workbook, and coauthor of the Every Man Bible studies. He is the area leader for men's ministry and teaches a men's interactive Bible study at Saddleback Church in Lake Forest, California. He and his wife, Chrissy, have three children and reside in Trabuco Canyon, California.

TODD WENDORFF is a graduate of University of California, Berkeley, and holds a ThM from Talbot School of Theology. He serves as a teaching pastor at King's Harbor Church in Redondo Beach and is an adjunct professor at Biola University. He is an author of the Doing Life Together Bible study series. Todd and his wife, Denise, live with their three children in Rolling Hills Estates, California.

start a bible study
and connect with others
who want to be God's man.

Every Man Bible Studies are designed to help you discover, own,
and build on convictions grounded in God's word.

WATERBROOK PRESS
www.waterbrookmultnomah.com

Printed in the United States
by Baker & Taylor Publisher Services